HOPE
Unbroken

A Book of Poetry For People Trying to Heal from Trauma

From the Growth From Darkness Collection

Amanda Blackwood

Healing is Hard.

Many people feel alone when they're going through the healing process after surviving something traumatic. I certainly did, and that's why I started writing so many years ago. The constant isolation left me with compounding health issues, both physical and mental. These days I've found much healthier ways to combat everything I'm going through, and I wanted to pass that along to you.

So I'm glad you have this book in your hands, and I'd love to hear your feedback either through an email or through leaving an honest review at your favorite online book retailer.

A book of poetry for people trying to heal from trauma

Part One: Fresh Pain

Hand in Worn Hand

Not a damsel, nor a ship lost at sea,
Yearning for a knight, a hero to set me free.
My strength, though battered, still flickers a flame,
I don't need a rescuer, just someone to name

The weight that I carry, the whispers of fear,
The storm in my silence, the unspoken tear.
Don't rush in with answers, with solutions so grand,
Just listen, intently, a hand reaching out, hand in hand.

My battles are mine, the scars I have earned,
A tapestry woven, a story discerned.
Don't try to erase them, don't paint them all gold,
Acknowledge the darkness, the truths yet untold.

Empathy's compass, a lighthouse in sight,
Guiding me homeward, through the darkest night.
Not a hero's glory, a trumpet's fanfare,
Just a listening ear, a soul that can care.

Of Little Comfort

They say time heals all wounds, a comforting refrain,
But the echoes of trauma whisper through my pounding brain.
I carry the weight of battles fought without a shield,
Scars that etch a story, battles lost, and battles yet revealed.

Anxiety, a serpent coiled tight around my chest,
Squeezing the air from my lungs, leaving me breathless.
The world a cacophony, a whirlwind out of control,
My mind a tangled forest, where reason loses its hold.

Exhaustion, a relentless tide that washes over me,
Dragging me down to the depths, where even dreams can't set me free.
The simplest tasks a mountain, a struggle to ascend,
My body a weary vessel, a fragile and failing friend.

Abuse, a poison sipped from a chalice laced with lies,
A twisted form of affection in those soulless, hollow eyes.
The sting of manipulation, the erosion of self-worth,
Left with a shattered reflection, a soul displaced from its birth.

Dangerous situations, a tightrope walk in the dark,
Every step a gamble, leaving an invisible mark.
The constant hum of fear, a cold sweat on my brow,
Wishing for solid ground, a place where I can avow:

I am only human, fragile and flawed, I confess.

Cracked but not broken, a warrior, nonetheless.
I have walked through fire, danced with the demons I knew,
And though the scars may linger, my spirit will pull me through.

I am the tremor that follows the earth's violent shake,
The resilience of a flower pushing through concrete to awake.
I am the tear that falls after the storm has passed,
The fragile hope that blossoms, stronger than the shadows cast.

I am the echo of thunder in a calming summer breeze,
The whisper of forgiveness carried on rustling leaves.
I am the flicker of a flame refusing to die,
The embers of defiance burning bright in my eye.

I am the space between shattered pieces, slowly piecing together,
A mosaic of resilience, in all kinds of weather.
I am the silent scream that finally finds its voice,
A testament to the human spirit, with an unwavering choice.

I am only human, but I will rise from the fray,
For even in the darkness, there's always a brighter day.
I will carry my burdens, but I won't be defined by the pain,
I will write my own story, etched in sunshine and rain.

Exhausts Us

The well that once brimmed with boundless might,
Feels parched and depleted, a well in the night.
The echoes of trauma, a persistent refrain,
Siphon my energy, leaving a dull, constant pain.
Exhaustion, a shroud, wraps heavy and tight,
Simple tasks a hurdle, a struggle for light.
A smile feels like climbing a treacherous peak,
And laughter, a whisper, too fragile to speak.
The world, a bright kaleidoscope, vibrant and loud,
But my senses are muted, lost in the crowd.
I yearn for a haven, a space to retreat,
Where silence can cradle, and slumber is sweet.
But even in slumber, the battles take hold,
Dreams twist and contort, stories left untold.
This exhaustion, a burden, a thief in the night,
But hope flickers faintly, a fragile, warm light.
For even the weariest warrior must rest,
To gather their strength, and put their pain to the test.
Self-care, a whisper, a promise I hold,
To mend the cracked vessel, to reclaim what was stolen.

On High Alert

Eyes scan the shadows, a constant ballet,
Searching for threats in the light of day.
Startled by sirens, a twitch at a sound,
Hypervigilance, a prison I've found.

My body remembers, a past etched in pain,
Always prepared for the storm's sudden rain.
Muscle tensed, senses on edge, never rest,
A hair-trigger reflex, a never-ending test.

Conversations muffled, a background I miss,
Lost in the analysis, every fleeting kiss.
Is that smile genuine, or a predator's grin?
The world's a performance, where danger creeps in.

Exhaustion a constant, a weight in my chest,
Yearning for moments my mind can finally rest.
But the switch stays on "flicker," a firefly's glow,
Always half-waiting for the bottom to go.

This is the trauma's echo, a haunting refrain,
But I won't let it silence the strength that remains.
With therapy's hand, and self-compassion's embrace,
I'll reclaim my peace, find a calmer space.

Share What You Need.

In the wreckage of yesterday's storm, a fragile heart remains,
Cracked but unbroken, whispering through the falling rain.
Scars etched like battle lines, a map of what they've faced,
But a flicker of resilience, a spirit not erased.

They need not empty platitudes, nor forced and hollow cheer,
Just a listening ear, a space where silent tears can appear.
A gentle hand to hold, a burden shared in two,
The solace of understanding, where empathy rings true.

Not pressure to "get over it," or timelines to erase,
But patience for the healing, a journey at their pace.
Permission to feel the anger, the hurt that lingers deep,
For grief must have its moment, before slumber and sweet sleep.

They need a quiet space to breathe, a refuge from the fray,
Where shattered pieces gather, and strength begins to play.
A chance to reconnect with self, the essence lost in strife,
To rediscover passions, and reclaim a vibrant life.

Not expectations to be whole, for healing isn't linear,

But acceptance of the journey, with moments both familiar and clearer.
For even fractured things can bloom, with sunlight and with care,
A testament to courage, a survivor standing there.

Disconnected.

A mirror held up,
But the face unknown,

A stranger stares back,
Where my laughter has flown.

Body a shell,
A hollowed out core,

The essence I was,
Lost in the war.

OUT

No forwarding address, this eviction's for keeps,
For the toxicity you sowed, the nightmares you reaped.
The door swings wide open, a draft of fresh air,
Banishing whispers, the burdens you'd share.

Out, manipulative charades, the gaslighting's done,
Out, the veiled threats and the battles half-won.
Out, the guilt trips and control, a tangled up web,
Out, the promises broken, the love that was bled.

This eviction notice, signed with a tear,
A testament to strength, a conquering cheer.
No longer a hostage to whispers and lies,
I reclaim my spirit, with truth in my eyes.

This space is now sacred, a haven of peace,
Where self-love can flourish, where kindness won't cease.
The echoes may linger, a ghost of the past,
But with each rising sun, the shadows won't last.

So go, uninvited, your presence a bane,
This eviction is permanent, etched clear in the rain.
I'll rewrite my story, with chapters brand new,
A survivor empowered, Stronger than you ever knew.

Healing From the Shadows

A shadow drapes my shoulders,
Unseen but ever near,
A constant hum of danger,
Whispering in my ear.
The world, a minefield hidden,
A smile with a hidden threat,
My senses on high alert,
A moment's peace, never met.
Laughter rings hollow,
A facade I must wear,
For fear is a serpent, coiled tight,
A constant, gnawing snare.
Startled by sudden touch,
A loud noise makes me flinch,
The past a recurring nightmare,
A relentless, painful pinch.
Hypervigilance my prison,
Scanning every space,
Seeking escape routes,
A frantic, never-ending race.
Trust, a fragile bird,
Hesitant to take flight,
Past betrayals echo,
Casting a chilling, endless night.
Longing for sanctuary,
A haven safe and sound,
But the world feels hostile,
On shaky, unsure ground.
Yearning for a day,
With peace as my embrace,

Where the shadow finally fades,
Leaving not a trace.

A Fractured Symphony: Dissociative Identity Disorder

A symphony unplayed, a chorus out of tune,
Melodies fragmented, beneath a painted moon.
We are the instruments, a fractured, hidden band,
Each holding a piece, of a story we can't withstand.

One hears the trauma's echo, a child's whimpered plea,
Another holds the anger, a raging, surging sea.
A protector stands guard, a shield against the pain,
While the core, the observer, watches through the rain.

We switch and we blend, a kaleidoscope's design,
Memories fragmented, a fractured timeline.
The world a blurred canvas, voices whispering low,
Who am I truly? This question we don't know.

But within the dissonance, a harmony we seek,
To join the fragments, a chorus strong and unique.
Acceptance and compassion, the notes we strive to play,
To heal the fractured symphony, and find a brighter day.

Late Nights

In the hush of the night, w
hen shadows hold sway,
My restless heart races,
sleep chooses to stray.
The world slumbers soundly,
while I fill the void,
A codependent dance,
a story unvoiced.
The phone's silent glow,
a beacon in the dark,
Awaiting a message,
a connection's stark spark.
Is someone out there,
needing me to see?
This fear of abandonment,
a constant decree.
Productivity beckons,
a mask for the chase,
Filling the silence
with tasks set in place.
But emails and deadlines,
a hollow display,
Can't mend the fractured self,
yearning for the day.
The moon, a pale witness,
to thoughts that take flight,
Obsessive ruminations,
fueling the night.
Lost in the validation,
a comment, a like,

A temporary fix,
for a soul on the bike.
But dawn's gentle fingers,
paint the sky with light,
Exposing the exhaustion,
the battle I fight.
This cycle must break,
a new path to explore,
To find solace within,
and need someone no more.

Silent Erosion

The world whispers traumas, some barely a breeze,
Yet they leave unseen scars on our hearts and our knees.
Microaggressions, a sting like a pin,
Dismissed as "no big deal," a place where hurt can begin.
Gaslighting's slow poison, a truth turned to doubt,
Our memories fractured, leaving us to shout,
"But this is what happened!" We plead and we fight,
But gaslighting's echo dims our inner light.
Emotional neglect, a void where love should reside,
A silent chill seeping, where warmth should confide.
"You're overreacting," the dismissive reply,
Ignoring the hunger, the silent, dry cry.
Medical gaslighting, dismissed as "all in your head,"
Chronic pain's burden, a truth left unsaid.
"It's just stress," they pronounce, with a dismissive wave,
Invalidating the struggle, the battle we crave.
These whispers of trauma, though subtle and sly,
Can erode our foundation, leave our spirit to die.
Let's break the silence, raise our voices in song,
Validate the unheard, where we truly belong.

Unscripted

A tangled web, this family of mine,
A play we perform, with lines pre-defined.
Each member a puppet, strings held tight,
Dancing a jig in the flickering light.

I, the scapegoat, the jester, the fool,
Assigned my role, expected to drool
Over their wisdom, their logic so skewed,
Acceptance a prize, if I played as I should.

Opinions unspoken, desires denied,
My voice, a mere whisper, easily defied.
Thoughts I expressed, met with withering stares,
Love turned to ice, a punishment for dares.

"You're too sensitive," their chorus would chime,
"Don't take things so hard," mocking the passage of time.
They painted my feelings a burden to bear,
A weight on their shoulders, a burden to share.

Secrets they hoarded, a truth buried deep,
A family portrait, where shadows do creep.
Dysfunction disguised, a performance so grand,
But truth, like a weed, will always expand.

When I dared to speak, to question the norm,
Love turned to fury, a brewing storm.
"You're tearing us apart!" they'd viciously claim,
Shifting the blame, a manipulative game.

Years of compliance, a dam holding tight,
But resentment grew, burning ever so bright.
The love I once craved, a twisted desire,
Conditional comfort, a flickering fire.

The dam finally burst, a flood of raw pain,
Words like a weapon, accusations like rain.
"This isn't a family," I screamed in the night,
"It's a cage built of lies, devoid of true light."

Silence descended, a heavy embrace,
Rejection a serpent, leaving its trace.
The love I once yearned for, a prize long decayed,
Replaced by a truth, a heart unafraid.

The path may be lonely, a journey unknown,
But freedom beckons, a place of my own.
I'll shed the old skin, the puppet's disguise,
Embrace my true self, with open, clear eyes.

This web I unravel, with courage I mend,
Building new connections, a love that transcends.
The ghosts of the past, I'll leave them behind,
Finding my voice, the strength of my kind.

For love shouldn't stifle, or punish, or bind,
True love is acceptance, a peace of the mind.
And though it may sting, this painful divorce,
It's the only way forward, to find my own course.

Fresh Pain

The weight of the world, a familiar friend,
Always a burden I carry, no end.
Sisyphus' toil, a climb ever steep,
Just reaching the peak, to fall back asleep.

A life etched in struggle, a battle long fought,
Victories fleeting, at dearly bought cost.
Now shadows grow longer, the path choked with thorns,
Health's fragile flame flickers, a future I mourn.

A question arises, a whisper so low,
"Is this all there is? Is it time to let go?"
The spirit grows weary, the will starts to fray,
The fight seems unending, will we see another day?

But deep in the embers, a flicker remains,
A stubborn defiance, a fire that strains.
A voice, though faint, whispers, "Hold on just tight,
For even in darkness, there can bloom hidden light."

So I gather the pieces, the strength that I hold,
And mend the frayed edges, a story untold.
This weight may be heavy, this battle unfair,
But I'll fight for one sunrise, one breath of fresh air.

The Face You See

A mask I wear, a smile both bright and bold,
A social grace to greet the passing day.
The world sees confidence, a story told
Of ease and joy, where shadows melt away.

But deep within, a tangled garden grows,
Where thorny doubts and fears like wild things creep.
A hidden world where vulnerability shows,
A well of tears the waking hours won't weep.

This public face, a shield against the storm,
Protects the fragile truth I hold so dear.
A whispered plea to keep my spirit warm,
A silent hope that someone might draw near.

For in the night, when masks at last are shed,
The truest self emerges from its bed.

The Real Healing Begins When

To flee the spark, the echo, or the sting,
A hollow shield against the rising tide,

Is but a dance where shadows intertwine,
A fragile peace by fleeting comfort tied.

The wound, unseen, festers in the dark,
A hidden beast that feeds on fear's command.

True healing blooms where triggers leave their mark,
A firestorm weathered, lessons held in hand.

Though pain may surge, a tempest in the soul,
Embrace the storm, confront the tangled thread.

For in the depths where buried stories roll,
A strength awakens, where new paths are tread.

Let scars be maps, not monuments of dread,
And walk your way, a future yet unsaid.

Soliloquy

(A weary sigh escapes, shoulders slumping)

The mirror mocks, a battleground displayed,
Dark circles etched where laughter once had stayed.
My body speaks, a symphony of woes,
Aching muscles, spirit's gentle throes.

Self-care, a whisper, lost in daily din,
A foreign land, where haven I can't win.
The tasks they beckon, deadlines loom and leer,
A siren song that drowns out inner cheer.

But whispers turn to shouts, a rising tide,
Demanding pause, where solace can reside.
A stolen breath, a moment carved with care,
A battlefield I fight, a burden hard to bear.

The bath beckons, a tepid, calming friend,
To wash away the day that knows no end.
Each gentle ripple, a whispered, soothing rhyme,
A lullaby to chase away lost time.

The book unread, a silent, patient friend,
Awaiting hands to turn the pages' end.
In worlds of fiction, worries lose their hold,
A stolen escape, a story yet untold.

The walk outside, a breath of fresh-kissed air,
Beneath the sun, a burden I can share.
The rustling leaves, a symphony so pure,
Nature's embrace, a gentle, healing cure.

Self-care, a battle fought on fragile ground,
Inch by painful inch, a victory is found.
For in the quiet moments, stolen and serene,
A stronger self emerges, a warrior unseen.

The mirror's gaze, no longer filled with dread,
Reflects a fighter, rising from the dead.
Self-care, a journey, not a single stop,
A path worth fighting for, never to drop.

Invisible Illnesses

In the grip of MCAS, a body under siege,
My husband's great burden, a stolen life's liege.

Energy sapped, a flicker, a spark,
Fun fades to longing for a nap in the dark.

Apologies echo, a chorus of shame,
For canceled adventures, a life out of frame.

The laughter I crave, replaced by a sigh,
Yearning for wellness, a tear in my eye.

But know that within, a fire still burns,
A love for connection, for all that life yearns.

Though fatigue may conquer, and shadows descend,
This bond ever strengthens, our friendship won't bend.

With hopeful whispers, I fight for each day,
For stolen embraces, for laughter with play.

Pray for the healing and the sunshine's return,
When laughter and energy will again brightly burn.

Though whispers of healing may linger as dreams,
A truth bittersweet, a current that gleams.

This path may not lead to a sunshine return,
But acceptance is comfort, I finally learned.

Let life surge and blossom, untamed and unbound,
With the strength that I gave you, & the love you have found.

Carry my spirit with a whisper, a breeze,
Don't pity me now! Just remember me, please.

Twice

Salt air stings my tear-streaked face
Newspapers flutter, a chilling embrace
"John, missing at sea," the headline screams
But the truth cuts deeper, a web of broken dreams

Your smile in a photo, a lover by your side
A life you built, a truth you tried to hide
Faked your final voyage, a cruel and twisted game
Now vengeance whispers your traitor's name

Anger, a fire that burns within my soul
Justice I will find, a story to be told
We'll sail the same waters, where you staged your escape
This time, the ending won't leave any room for mistake

The boat creaks and groans, a storm begins to brew
Your eyes widen with fear, as your past catches up to you
A push, a splash, the waves swallow you whole
Your screams are silenced, a story to be told

Silence descends, a heavy, chilling weight
The taste of victory, quickly turns to hate
Justice served cold, a twisted kind of peace
But the serpent of doubt starts slowly to increase

The guilt, a tide that rises in my chest
Can vengeance erase the love we once professed?
A life for a life, a debt I can't repay
The haunted wife, forever and a day

Sun peeks through the window, birdsong fills the air
The sheets tangled beside me, a weight I can't bear
 A gasp escapes my lips, a cold sweat on my brow
It was all a nightmare, thank God, you're here now.

My eyes flutter once more and I realize it's a dream.
My vision swims, the scene distorts, a figment it would seem.
Are you there? The silence stretches into the unknown.
The fear creeps in, I'm afraid to see if I'm alone.

Caught in the Current

A tug-of-war within, a ceaseless strife,
Pulled forward, backward, in the ebb and flow of life.
A tempest rages, where shadows creep and hide,
Fear's icy fingers, where courage ought to abide.

To step into the light, a daunting quest,
Where healing's promise, hope's gentle rest.
But shadows whisper, of danger lurking near,
Of wounds still open, and echoes of fear.

The heart, a compass, seeking true north's gleam,
Yet caught in undertow, a haunting dream.
To break free from the chains, a valiant fight,
To embrace the future, with newfound light.

With measured steps, we navigate the shore,
Finding balance, where we've stumbled before.
Each wave retreats, revealing sandy ground,
A place to anchor, where strength can be found.

So let us journey, with courage as our guide,
Through stormy waters, where fears subside.
And in this push and pull, we'll find our way,
To a calmer ocean, where hope will stay.

In the Undertow
(A Continuation of
Caught in the Current)

A battle waged within, a silent war,
To step into the light, or close the door.
The heart, a compass, seeking steady ground,
While fear's tempestuous waves come crashing round.

To heal and grow, a tender, fragile seed,
Nurtured by courage, in desperate need.
Yet shadows loom, of pain and dark despair,
A haunting echo, of what once was there.

Each step forward, a victory won,
A battle chosen, when the day is done.
To find the balance, between hope and dread,
A delicate dance, where strength is bred.

With every breath, a choice to make anew,
To face the future, or the past to pursue.
And in this journey, where shadows intertwine,
May inner peace and resilience shine.

For in the depths, a flicker of light,
A beacon calling, through the darkest night.
And with each step, we find our way,
To a place of healing, come what may.

Lost in the Labyrinth

A child, a fortress, built against the storm,
A tender soul encased in walls of steel.
No time for dreams, where shadows dark inform
A world of chaos, where wounds deeply heal.
Survival's task, a constant, weary fight,
To navigate a minefield, step by step.
No room for wonder, joy, or pure delight,
Just endless vigil, where shadows creep.
And so they grow, with armor worn and frayed,
A stranger to themselves, a hollow shell.
The child within, suppressed, afraid,
A prisoner of echoes, where nightmares dwell.
To find their essence, buried deep inside,
A journey arduous, where courage will abide.

To peel back layers, like an onion's skin,
To unearth the self, a fragile, tender seed.
A labyrinth of pain, where they've been confined,
A maze of shadows, where true selves recede.
With trembling hands, they seek a guiding light,
To illuminate the corners, dark and deep.
To claim their power, with renewed might,
From trauma's depths, where memories sleep.
And slowly, gently, they begin to mend,
To piece together fragments of their soul.
With every step, a newfound friend,
To face the demons, make themselves whole.
For in the heart of darkness, hope endures,
A flame ignited, where healing ensures.

Please Don't Say It

To call me strong, a hollow, empty praise,

For strength implies a choice, a conscious stand.

Yet I was trapped in horror's endless maze,

A helpless vessel in another's hand.

Survival, not a badge of valor worn,

But mere existence in a world of dread.

To say I'm strong, my spirit is forlorn,

For strength is forged in battles bravely led.

I yearned for freedom, longed to break the chains,

But fear's cold grip held fast upon my heart.

So spare me now these well-intended strains,

Of strength and courage, torn apart.

I am a survivor, yes, it's true,

But I'm no hero, even to you.

A book of poetry for people trying to heal from trauma

A book of poetry for people trying to heal from trauma

Part Two:
Half Way
Through

Claustrophobia of the Soul

Claustrophobia of the soul, a cage built from within,
Walls of fear constricting, where freedom used to grin.
A trauma's cruel echo, a whispered, haunting plea,
"There's no escape," it murmurs, "no key to set you free."

The world shrinks to a corner, a canvas painted gray,
Possibilities vanish, replaced by yesterday.
Flight or fight, the choices blur in a panicked haze,
Frozen by the memory, trapped in a mental maze.

But this, dear heart, remember, is a trauma's bitter hold,
A defense mechanism, a story yet untold.
The cage may feel real, the bars cold and unyielding,
But you are not the captive, your spirit's fire is wielding.

With time and gentle healing, the walls begin to bend,
Cracks appear in the darkness, a light you can ascend.

You'll breathe again, feel open, the world a canvas bright,
And step out of the shadows, bathed in hope's gentle light.

Remember to Rest

The shadows linger beneath your tired eyes,
A flicker of exhaustion, a weary disguise.

But rest, dear friend, comes in more than one guise,
So tell me, what kind of solace would bring sweet surprise?

Is it silence you crave, a haven from sound?
A gentle escape where worries can't be found?

Or perhaps a distraction, a laughter-filled spree,
To chase away troubles with lighthearted glee?

Maybe a long walk, the rhythm of feet,
Connecting with nature, a calming retreat.

Or a creative outlet, a brushstroke so bold,
To spill out your feelings, a story untold?

Perhaps it's a shoulder, a comforting hand,
To share the weight of burdens, to understand.

Or a warm cup of tea, a moment to unwind,
Simple pleasures to soothe and ease your mind.

Don't hesitate to speak, let your needs unfold,
For the perfect type of rest is often a story untold.

Calm the Storm

The waves of emotion crash, a relentless, angry tide,
Threatening to pull me under, where reason can't reside.

But in this frantic chaos, tools I've learned take hold,
Distress tolerance whispers, a story yet untold.

T.I.P.P., a beacon bright, cutting through the fog,
Temperature shift, a splash of cool, a calming dog.

Intense exercise, a sprint, a burst of channeled might,
Paced breathing, in and out, reclaiming inner light.

A.C.C.E.P.T.S., the storm I face, with open, gentle eye,
Acknowledge the feelings, where truth and vulnerability lie.

Commit to staying present, in this moment, here and now,
Connect with the senses, the world somehow feels new.

Effectiveness of coping, the skills I've come to trust,
Push away the judgments, for self-compassion I must.

IMPROVE the situation, if action can be found,
P.R.O.S. and CONS weighed carefully, on solid ground.

Self-soothe with kindness, a mantra whispered low,
"This too shall pass," the seeds of hope begin to sow.

These are the life rafts in the storm, the anchors in the fray,

Distress tolerance whispers, guiding me on my way.

Invisible Illness

They whisper, "Just get up, it can't be that bad,"
But the weight of exhaustion makes my very soul sad.
It's not laziness, this heavy cloak I wear,
It's the residue of battles, a burden hard to bear.

My mind, a battlefield where anxieties collide,
Leaving scars of sleepless nights, where peace is hard to find.
My body, a weary soldier, muscles screaming in protest,
Every simple movement feels like pushing against a crest.

This exhaustion isn't sloth, it's the echo of past storms,
The lingering whispers of trauma, keeping me out of forms.
It's the weight of unseen battles, fought in the silent night,
A constant undertow, dragging me from the light.

But know this, dear world, though I may seem to rest,
My spirit's not defeated, within my tired chest
Burns a flicker of defiance, a fire that won't expire,
I'll rise again, resurface, fueled by a hidden pyre.

So judge not my stillness, for within it lies the fight,
The struggle to reclaim my strength, and step back into the light.
For even warriors need respite, a chance to mend and heal,
To gather the fragments, and make their spirit whole and real.

A Mighty Soft Roar

A voice, though small,
Finds rising tide,

No longer swept
By shadows' hide.

My truth I speak,
My ground I claim,

Respect
Deserves

A
  Whispered
    Name.

Criticism Accord

A childhood of whispers, a constant refrain,
"Not good enough," a mantra, etched deep in my brain.
Every stumble a spotlight, a chorus of blame,
Shame as a shroud, extinguishing life's flame.

Mirrors once portals, reflecting a foe,
Imperfections magnified, a soul laid too low.
Judgment, a hammer, relentless and crude,
Shattering confidence, misunderstood.

Words, like barbed wire, constricting and tight,
Choking creativity, dimming my inner light.
The space for exploration, shrunken and small,
Living in fear of missteps, a constant freefall.

But whispers now fading, a strength starts to rise,
Unlearning the echoes, with truth in my eyes.
Rewriting the narrative, with compassion's embrace,
Shedding the shackles, finding my rightful place.

These scars, a reminder, of battles I've won,
A testament to resilience, a journey begun.
No longer a mirror that reflects their disdain,
But a canvas for growth, in the pouring rain.

Struggle Onward!

The world throws punches, a relentless fight,
Muscles burning, grasping for light.
Stumbles and falls, a teetering pace,
Does struggle equate to a shameful disgrace?

No, my friend, for within the fray,
Strength is unveiled in a different way.
The effort expended, the will to keep going,
These are the embers of triumph still glowing.

A sculptor with chisel, each chip and each crack,
Marks the path to a masterpiece, never looking back.
A seed underground, pushing through stone,
Becomes a magnificent oak, standing proudly alone.

So let the tears fall, a cleansing rain,
Washing away doubts, and easing the strain.
Embrace the struggle, a fire's embrace,
Forging resilience, leaving no space.

For failure's dark whispers, a thief in the night.
You rise with the dawn, bathed in hopeful light.
This journey's a climb, with twists and with turns,
But the summit awaits, where your spirit still burns.

The Phantoms of Danger Still Linger Within

This vessel, my body, a fortress so keen,
Remembers the battles, the struggles unseen.
Though peace has descended, a war long since done,
Phantom alarms echo, the fight's not quite won.
A shadow approaches, a memory's sting,
Heart hammers a rhythm, a frantic bird's wing.
Sweat beads on my forehead, a primal, cold dread,
Though safety surrounds me, the danger long dead.
Muscles tense, ready, a coiled viper's might,
Breath comes in gasps, a desperate flight.
The body remembers the predator's call,
Though reason whispers, "No harm can befall."
This loyal defender, this guardian wise,
Still locked in the past, with fear-filled eyes.
It fights for survival, a duty so deep,
Though wounds have healed over, the memories creep.
But slowly, we'll teach it, a message so clear,
The danger is distant, the coast truly clear.
With gentle compassion, with mindful embrace,
We'll retrain the response, find a calmer space.

Delayed Realization

The fog lifts slow, a distant shore appears,
A land I left, yet clung to with blind tears.
Years spent in shadows, whispers in the night,
Believing darkness somehow held the light.

The heart, a compass spun by a twisted hand,
North pointed nowhere, lost in shifting sand.
Love's tender language twisted, warped, and frayed,
My voice a whisper, spirit half-decayed.

But freedom's breath, a gentle, cleansing breeze,
Parts the thick veil, and truth begins to tease.
The echoes soften, memories replayed,
The blame unveiled, the cost I've truly paid.

Each harsh decree, each flicker of disdain,
Each stolen dream, a symphony of pain.
The justifications crumble, built on lies,
A haunting echo in apology-filled eyes.

The fog recedes, the landscape stands defined,
A path of scars left etched upon my mind.
But with each step, the burden feels less dire,
The strength to heal, a slowly kindling fire.

This delayed awakening, a bitter sting,
Yet freedom's dawn, a hopeful song to sing.
For even broken compasses, with time, can mend,
And point the way to where true love can send.

Strength in Tears

Not in the forced smile, the glistening tear,
Nor silence that hides a heart full of fear,
Does true strength reside, a warrior's might.
It's in the voice that speaks through the darkest night.

The mask of composure, a burden so grand,
Cracks under pressure, a shifting sand.
Strength isn't numbness, a stoic façade,
It's the courage to say, "I'm hurting, I'm sad."

The tears that they fall, a cleansing rain,
Washing away the burdens, the unspoken pain.
In vulnerability, a power untold,
A strength that connects, braver than gold.

So let the emotions, like rivers, flow free,
Share the weight you carry, and finally be.
For strength isn't silence, it's the battle you fight,
To speak your truth, and step into the light.

Echoes of Then

A sudden storm in a sunlit space,
A memory's grip, a distorted embrace.
Emotional flashbacks, they come and they go,
Leaving a trail of confusion and woe.
Disproportionate the reaction may seem,
A trigger ignites, a shattered dream.

A raised voice, a slamming door,
A whisper of fear from a life long before.
The present dissolves, a stage set aflame,
We're pulled back to then, reliving the blame.
Heart pounding, breath hitched, a primal despair,
The past bleeds into now, a burden to bear.

A sudden surge of emotions untold,
Fear, anger, and sadness, a story unfolds.
The body remembers, the scars etched deep,
Trapped in a moment we desperately seek
To escape, to rewind, to erase and rewrite,
But the flashback holds tight, a suffocating night.

We lash out, we withdraw, a desperate plea,
To push away the ghost we long to be free.
Lashing out in words, a defensive display,
Protecting ourselves from the shadows at play.
Misunderstood actions, a bridge burned in haste,
The cost of the flashback, a future embraced

By guilt and regret, a burden we hold,
Feeling unfit for the stories untold.

The weight of the past, a constant refrain,
Can we ever escape the echoing pain?
Inconsistent the pattern, a thief in the night,
A trigger unseen, igniting a fight.

The world fades away, replaced by a scene,
A distorted reality, a trauma so keen.
But through the storm clouds, a sliver of light,
The knowledge we're healing, with all of our might.
These flashbacks, a reminder, a battle we face,
But with self-compassion, we'll find our own space.

Struggle

Yes, this poem,
A piece of me.
Yes, this photo,
A memory.
Yes, the cycle,
Ever the same,
Yes, the struggle,
A whispered name.
Yes, the depths
I once did know,
Yes, the strength
To still outflow.
Yes, the mask
I wear with a smile,
Yes, I'm alright,
For a little while.

Cautious Joy

The scars remain, a map of battles won,
Where shadows lurked and battles had been done.
No longer raw, they hold a softer trace,
A testament to time's erasing grace.

The echoes fade, the whispers lose their sting,
No longer nightmares make the night owls sing.
The shattered mind begins to mend and sew,
A tapestry of strength where weakness grew.

The tears still fall, a cleansing, gentle rain,
But wash away the burdens and the pain.
A fragile trust is built on shaky ground,
In connections safe, where solace can be found.

The laughter rings, a melody reborn,
No longer choked by fear, or emotions shorn.
A cautious joy, a tentative embrace,
A fragile bloom in a once barren space.

For healing's path is slow, a winding road,
But hope remains, a heavy burden bode.
With every step, the darkness loses hold,
And light emerges, making stories told.

Fourfold Response

Flight, fight, freeze, or fawn, a primal art,
Survival's compass, etched deep in the heart.
No blame, no shame, in how we react,
For each response is a sturdy, strong fact.

When fear's cold hand upon the soul does creep,
These instincts rise, from slumbering deep.
To flee the storm, or face it with might,
Or stillness embrace, in the darkest of night.

Or tend to another, to soften the blow,
A shield of compassion, where wounds may grow.
Each path is valid, a choice of the mind,
Shaped by experiences, uniquely defined.

To judge another's course, it's a grave mistake,
For empathy's the bridge that we should create.
"I would have done this," a harmful decree,
Ignoring the depths of another's decree.

For who can truly know what lies within,
The silent struggles, the unseen sin?
So let us honor the spirit's defense,
And offer support, with gentle essence.

For in understanding, healing can start,
As we mend the fractures, one open heart.

Dualities of Healing

I walk a path of shadows and of light,
A winding road where contradictions reside.
Progress made, yet echoes of the night
Still haunt my dreams, where wounded spirits hide.

I've learned to voice my needs, a fragile sound,
A whisper in the wind, a tentative plea.
Yet fear of rejection, deeply underground,
Can silence me, and set my spirit free.

I yearn for connection, a soulful embrace,
To trust another, to open wide my heart.
But shadows of abandonment still trace
Their mournful patterns, tearing me apart.

I strive for patience, understanding's grace,
To see the flaws in others, human art.
Yet expectations linger, a haunting case,
A silent judge within my weary heart.

I've found my strength, a flicker in the dark,
A growing flame that pushes through the night.
And yet, I stumble, falter, lose my mark,
And drown in self-doubt, with all my might.

I'm healing, growing, changing every day,
A garden tended, where new blossoms bloom.
But weeds of trauma still find a way,
To choke the tender shoots, cast them in gloom.

It's in this tension, where I find my peace,
A balance sought, a delicate art.
To hold two truths, without reprieve or cease,
And carry on, with a courageous heart.

I'm strong and vulnerable, hopeful and afraid,
A complex tapestry, woven through and through.
And in this journey, I'm slowly being made,
A new creation, with a purpose true.

I'm learning to accept, without harsh decree,
The imperfections within, and those around.
To grant myself compassion, wild and free,
And find my center, on sacred ground.

So let me celebrate the steps I've taken,
The miles I've traveled, the mountains I've climbed.
And let me honor the shadows that awaken,
The fears and doubts that often feel unkind.

For in this dance of light and darkest night,
I'm finding strength, resilience, and grace.
To live in paradox, with all my might,
And claim my healing, at my own slow pace.

Part Three: Feeling the Healing

Emotional Cup

The heart, a brimming cup, a chalice overflowing,
With laughter's sweet nectar and joy everflowing.
Gratitude's warmth simmers, a current that churns,
As kindness and empathy in gentle flame burn.

Passion, a heady wine, a vibrant crimson hue,
Infuses each moment, a vibrant, soulful view.
Forgiveness, a clear spring, washes clean every scar,
Leaving room for new feelings, no longer too far.

But beware, for the cup, though robust, has its brim,
Let anger's hot embers not overflow and swim.
Sadness, a heavy rain, can cloud and obscure,
Leaving a taste of bitterness, a spirit less pure.

So find a wise balance, let emotions all flow,
But nurture the positive, let negativity go.
Share your cup's bounty, with those in your sight,
For hearts overflowing create a world ever bright.

Song Without a Tune

(Verse 1)
Stole me outta nowhere, shipped me like a dime
Empty promises whispered, stealin' my sunshine
Darkness pressed around me, felt like I would drown
But deep inside a fire burned, a fightin' kind of sound
(Chorus)
Trafficked, broken, yeah, they thought they won
But I'm a hurricane comin', stronger than the sun
Got my story writ in ink, my voice will rise above
This survivor's anthem, a song of fearless love
(Verse 2)
Fought like a lioness caged, refused to be their game
Every tear I shed, the fire only grew with flame
Escaped the cage they built me, ran beneath the stars
Now I'm speakin' out for all those who're trapped behind
those bars
(Chorus)
Trafficked, broken, yeah, they thought they won
But I'm a hurricane comin', stronger than the sun
Got my story writ in ink, my voice will rise above
This survivor's anthem, a song of fearless love
(Bridge)
Scars on my body, a map of where I've been
But they don't define me, they're the battles I have win
(Chorus)
Trafficked, broken, yeah, they thought they won
But I'm a hurricane comin', stronger than the sun
Got my story writ in ink, my voice will rise above
This survivor's anthem, a song of fearless love

(Outro)
This is my victory song, my liberation cry
Hear it echo through the world, watch the darkness die
I'm a survivor, a warrior, and I will not be beat
This is my survivor's anthem, the power of the street.

Self Care is Selfless

Not mirrors that judge, nor whispers that doubt,
My worth isn't measured by accolades' shout.
I stand on my own, with a heart that feels true,
My compass within, a me I can accrue.

The stumbles and falls, the lessons I've learned,
Have woven a tapestry, beautifully earned.

The cracks in my soul, where resilience resides,
Speak louder than failures, where strength now confides.

No longer dependent on praise or acclaim,
My validations are a whisper, a self-loving flame.
For progress, not perfection, is what sets me free,
The journey's the treasure, the best version of me.

So let the applause fade, the judgments depart,
My spirit's a fortress, a work of brave art.

I am enough, worthy, with flaws and with grace,
This self-love embrace, a beautiful space.

Happy Chemicals

Not potions nor pills, but a symphony to play,
Of actions and choices that brighten your day.
Dopamine dances when goals you achieve,
So conquer that challenge, and truly believe.

Oxytocin's warmth in connection you'll find,
With loved ones who cherish, a bond that's entwined.
A hug or a cuddle, a heart-to-heart chat,
These moments ignite the love that just can't be sat on.

Serotonin soars with the sun's golden ray,
A walk in the park, or a stroll by the bay.
Embrace the outdoors, let nature's embrace,
Fill you with sunshine and leave not a trace

Endorphins erupt when your body's in flow,
From a vigorous workout, a rhythmic head-to-toe.
Dance like no one's watching, or run with the breeze,
This happy release brings you sweet inner peace.

So listen to your body, its whispers and cries,
For these healthy habits bring sunshine to your eyes.
Dopamine, Oxytocin, Serotonin, Endorphins too,
A symphony of joy, just waiting for you!

I Am Only Human

Anxiety, a serpent coiled tight around my chest,
Squeezing the air from my lungs, leaving me breathless.
The world a cacophony, a whirlwind out of control,
My mind a tangled forest, where reason loses its hold.

Exhaustion, a relentless tide that washes over me,
Dragging me down to the depths, where even dreams can't set me free.
The simplest tasks a mountain, a struggle to ascend,
My body a weary vessel, a fragile and failing friend.

Abuse, a poison sipped from a chalice laced with lies,
A twisted form of affection in those soulless, hollow eyes.
The sting of manipulation, the erosion of self-worth,
Left with a shattered reflection, a soul displaced from its birth.

Dangerous situations, a tightrope walk in the dark,
Every step a gamble, leaving an invisible mark.
The constant hum of fear, a cold sweat on my brow,
Wishing for solid ground, a place where I can avow:

I am only human, fragile and flawed, I confess.Cracked but not broken, a warrior, nonetheless.I have walked through fire, danced with the demons I knew,And though the scars may linger, my spirit will pull me through.

I am the tremor that follows the earth's violent shake,
The resilience of a flower pushing through concrete to awake.

I am the tear that falls after the storm has passed,
The fragile hope that blossoms, stronger than the shadows cast.

I am the echo of thunder in a calming summer breeze,
The whisper of forgiveness carried on rustling leaves.
I am the flicker of a flame refusing to die,
The embers of defiance burning bright in my eye.

I am the space between shattered pieces, slowly piecing together,
A mosaic of resilience, in all kinds of weather.
I am the silent scream that finally finds its voice,
A testament to the human spirit, with an unwavering choice.

I am only human, but I will rise from the fray,
For even in the darkness, there's always a brighter day.
I will carry my burdens, but I won't be defined by the pain,
I will write my own story, etched in sunshine and rain.

Source of Love

My heart, a dialect shaped by silent years,
Speaks a language of acts, not whispered endearments,
dear.
For affirmations hung heavy, unspoken and cold,
Leaving a void where affection's warmth should unfold.

So, I crave the language of deeds, not of praise,
A helping hand extended through life's winding maze.
A shared burden lightens, a silent support unseen,
Speaks volumes louder than words, a love that's ever
keen.

Comfort in quiet presence, a haven from the storm,
A shoulder to lean on, a space to keep me warm.
These are the phrases that resonate most true,
A language built from absence, a love that's fiercely new.

Empty plates speak louder than empty words of care,
So acts of service become the language I most share.
A meal prepared with love, a chore silently done,
These whispers of devotion, the battles I've already won.

Perhaps a touch lingers, a brush of hands so brief,
A fleeting moment that speaks volumes of relief.
For physical affection, a language seldom known,
Blooms hesitantly, a seed carefully sown.

Gifts, not of trinkets, but of time and gentle thought,
A moment carved out, a battle bravely fought.
These are the love letters my heart yearns to write,

A testament to longing, bathed in a gentle light.

They say love languages are learned, a dialect we choose,
But mine's a reflection of what I never used.
A silent yearning, a longing to connect,
In the space between absences, a love I now detect.

So listen closely, not to words that may not come,
But to the whispers of action, the love that overcomes.
For my heart speaks a language born of what was missed,
A love that blooms in silence, a love that can't be dismissed.

Today's Reminders

The voice whispers, a serpent's hiss,
"You don't deserve this, not after this."

It coils around comfort, a chilling embrace,
A relic of trauma, haunting this space.

But listen, dear heart, a truth I impart,
Self-care isn't a luxury, but a healing art.
The battles you fought, the burdens you bore,
Deserve gentle tending, a chance to restore.

The bath isn't selfish, a moment to unwind,
To soothe the spent muscles, and leave worries behind.

The rest isn't weakness, a space to recharge,
To gather your strength, to turn back the large.

The quiet reflection, not a waste of time,
A chance to reconnect, to piece back the rhyme.
The tears that you shed, not a sign of defeat,
A cleansing release, a bittersweet treat.

Those boundaries you set, a shield, not a wall,
Protecting your spirit, preventing a fall.

The "no" you say firmly, a right you reclaim,
Respecting your limits, whispering self-love's name.

The voice may still echo, a lingering doubt,
But drown it with kindness, let compassion shout.

You are worthy of care, in every small way,
For even a warrior deserves a peaceful day.

So breathe in the sunlight, let worries take flight,
Embrace the indulgence, a healing, soft light.

For self-care isn't a burden, but a gentle embrace,
A survivor's right, to find a loving space.

Self-Energy

The flame flickers low, a whisper in the breeze,
But embers still smolder, a chance for inner ease.

To fan the dying light, a path we must pave,
With simple steps, dear soul, your energy you can save.

First, heed the body's call, in slumber find your rest.
Let worries drift away, on dreams put to the test.

A mind renewed and clear, a body strong and whole,
Forms the foundation firm, to reach your destined goal.

Next, nourish from the earth, let vibrant colors bloom.
Fruits and greens abound, dispel the inner gloom.

Hydration's vital stream, keep the wellspring full,
Fueling every action, a revitalizing pull.

Move your weary limbs, let gentle breezes blow.
A walk beneath the sun, or yoga's graceful flow.

Stretch and breathe deeply, awaken slumbering might,
For movement stirs the spirit, and sets the darkness right.

Disconnect, dear friend, from screens' incessant hum.
Silence nurtures silence, lets inner voices come.

Nature's symphony, a balm for weary ears,
Quietude's embrace, dispelling hidden fears.

Lastly, fill your cup with joy, with things that make you smile.
A cherished hobby practiced, for just a little while.

Laughter's medicine sweet, a lightness in the soul,
Renewing inner fire, to make you feel whole.

So listen to your body, its wisdom whispers true,
With gentle self-care, your energy renews.

Amazing, Beautiful, Love

Your smile, a spark that ignites the room,
Warmth radiating, chasing away gloom.
A gentle word, a listening ear,

Easing burdens, dispelling fear.
Laughter rings, a symphony bright,
Shared moments of joy, taking flight.

Creativity blooms, a vibrant display,
Inspiring others to light up their day.
With open arms, you embrace the world,

Compassionate spirit, forever unfurled.
A bridge you build, hearts to connect,
Leaving a trail where shadows retract.

Amazing in your ability to uplift,
Inspiring others to make a joyful shift.
Positive energy, a contagious delight,

Bringing sunshine on even the darkest night.
You are the difference, a beacon so bold,
A story of kindness, beautifully told.

Permission to Bloom

Not carved in stone, these lines we walk,
Not tethered tight, a whispered talk.
These walls we built, of fear and doubt,
Can crumble down, with strength devout.

They told you "No," a chilling sound,
For needs expressed, on hallowed ground.
But buried deep, a yearning true,
A right to ask, a right to you.

No longer chained by twisted tongue,
Your voice can rise, a joyful song.
Unfurl the flag of what you need,
Plant boundaries, a fertile seed.

"It's selfish," they may try to say,
But self-respect lights up your way.
For love that thrives is built on care,
Where both can breathe the open air.

Permission blooms, a gentle flower,
No longer bound by their dark power.
Embrace your wants, with open hand,
You are allowed, to take a stand.

This life you hold, a precious thing,
Deserving joy, on soaring wing.
So let your needs, like banners fly,
Allowed to ask, allowed to try.

Thirteen Years

Thirteen years, a stolen time,
A shadow cast, a broken rhyme.
Escaped the grip, the cruel decree,
But freedom's song held no guarantee.

For scars remained, whispers of fear,
Could anyone love what once held tears?
A shattered soul, a fragile thing,
Would acceptance ever take wing?

Then doubt took flight, on wings of blue,
The day I met a man so true.
Kyle, with eyes that held the sun,
Saw not the past, but battles won.

His love, a balm, a gentle hand,
Healed the wounds in this broken land.
With patience sown, and trust reborn,
A love so fierce, weathered every storm.

Today, we stand, a testament bold,
Love's tapestry, a story told.
No longer lost, no longer scared,
With Kyle by my side, a life declared.

Thirteen years,
A distant shore,
But love's embrace,
Forevermore.

Learning to Communicate

Across the chasm, a bridge we yearn to mend,
A sea of words, where meaning can transcend.
But tangled tongues and careless phrases fly,
Leaving hearts wounded, beneath a tearful sky.

Oh, to connect, a symphony of souls,
Where empathy resonates, and understanding unfolds.
Let intent be clear, a beacon in the storm,
No hidden barbs, to cause emotional harm.

Choose words with care, like jewels upon a thread,
Each one a promise, carefully to be read.
Speak with kindness, for voices have the power,
To build a fortress, or dismantle in an hour.

Listen with your heart, not just your ears alone,
The unspoken whispers, a tender, mournful tone.
See through the eyes of another, feel their plight,
For true connection blossoms in the empathetic light.

And when the conversation fades, a seed is sown,
Follow through with actions, to let your feelings be known.
A simple gesture, a hand upon the shoulder's hold,
Speaks volumes more than empty words, once told.

For communication's dance, a delicate ballet,
Requires mindful steps, each moving the right way.
With honest intent, and words that truly care,
We bridge the gap, and hearts in harmony, we share.

Communicate

Words take flight,
like birds on wings,
But meaning lost,
confusion stings.
A bridge we build
with every phrase,
Misunderstood,
it crumbles in a daze.
Listen close,
with heart and mind,
The message true,
you'll surely find.
Speak with care,
let kindness guide,
For careless words
can wound inside.
Empathy's touch,
a gentle art,
Connects the souls,
and mends the heart.

Keep Talking

Upon the wind, a message rides unseen,
A fragile thread 'tween spirits wild and keen.
But tangled oft, the meaning takes its flight
Leaving a void where understanding's light
Should brightly burn. Thus, heed these lessons well,
Five guiding stones, a tale for thee to tell.
First, tend the flame of purpose in thy breast,
Ere words take flight, let clarity be dressed.
For aimless thoughts, like smoke, will drift away,
No solace found on this bewildering way.
Then, choose with care the weapons of thy tongue,
Each syllable a weight, both fierce and young.
Let kindness sheath the point of every barb,
Lest trust be slain, a fragile, wounded barb.
With open ears, a listening spirit seek,
For whispers soft, the truths the heart can speak.
Beyond the words, a deeper music lies,
Where empathy's embrace compassion ties.
When words have flown, and silence fills the air,
Let actions true the weight of language bear.
A hand outstretched, a promise to fulfill,
These bind the threads, where hearts and minds stand still.
Thus, with these tools, a bridge of souls you'll weave,
Where understanding's light shall brightly cleave
The veil of doubt. Let clarity ignite,
And hearts entwined, in purest converse write.

Ember of Hope

The path of healing, long and fraught with woe,
Winds through a landscape scarred by battles long ago.
The ghosts of trauma linger, whispers faint,
Of shattered dreams and battles fought in paint.

But hope, a flickering ember, yet remains,
Fueled by the will to break these mental chains.
With trembling hands, the wounded soul must mend,
Each fragile piece, a story without end.

The tears that fall, a cleansing, bitter rain,
Wash clean the wounds, and ease the searing pain.
The scars they leave, a testament to strife,
But also strength, a will to rise from life.

Forgiveness sought, a burden to release,
From those who wronged, or those who brought no peace.
A gift of grace, not for the one who erred,
But for oneself, a freedom long deferred.

With gentle steps, the path begins to mend,
As love and laughter slowly reascend.
The shattered mind, once fractured and afraid,
Embraces joy, a life anew displayed.

The journey's long, with trials yet to face,
But hope remains, a guiding, steady grace.
For trauma's hold, though strong, can yet be frayed,

And in the scars, a strength forever stayed.

Phoenix Rising

From ashes of pain, a phoenix I've grown,
A masterpiece forged, a spirit unknown.
Molded by fire, tempered by strife,
Emerged stronger, claiming my life.

No longer a captive, a shadow's disguise,
I gaze into depths of my own, clear eyes.
With courage as armor, I step into light,
Embracing this moment, with all of my might.

The old self has faded, a distant refrain,
Replaced by a warrior, who's conquered the pain.
A tapestry woven with threads of resilience,
A heart full of hope, a spirit immense.

I am a survivor, a story untold,
With scars as reminders, my spirit has grown bold.
No longer defined by the darkness I've seen,
I am a new dawn, a hope-filled queen.

So let us embrace, this beautiful art,
A masterpiece crafted, right from the start.
With every heartbeat, a victory's won,
A phoenix reborn, beneath the sun.

Choice and Kindness

Happiness, a fleeting guest, it seems,
A willful bird that soars beyond our reach.
We chase its shadow through ethereal dreams,
But find it elusive, a fragile speech.

Yet, in this darkness, a choice remains,
A gentle path to tread, a softer ground.
To turn inward, soothe our aching pains,
With kindness offered, healing can be found.

We cannot mandate joy, or force a smile,
When sorrow's weight upon our spirits lies.
But in this moment, for a little while,
We can be tender with ourselves, wise.

To offer solace, comfort, and a friend,
A listening ear, a compassionate bend.
Though storms may rage, and shadows descend,
Inner peace is ours, to cultivate and tend.

Help is Available.

The road to healing after trauma is rarely a solitary path. While facing a traumatic experience can feel isolating, attempting recovery without support can be a dangerous gamble. Trauma leaves deep scars, both emotional and psychological, and navigating them alone can lead to a path of deeper suffering.

One of the biggest challenges of solo recovery is the risk of denial. Trauma can be overwhelming, and pushing down the experience can feel like a way to cope. However, denial hinders true healing. Memories and emotions resurface eventually, often triggered by seemingly unrelated events, leading to confusion and emotional turmoil.

Trauma can also disrupt our sense of safety and trust. Trying to rebuild this foundation alone can be a daunting task. Without a safe space to process the experience and its aftermath, survivors may become hypervigilant, constantly scanning their environment for threats. This can lead to anxiety, social isolation, and a distorted view of the world.

Another danger of solo recovery is self-destructive coping mechanisms. Trauma can leave a deep well of emotional pain, and some may turn to substances or risky behaviors to numb the ache. These behaviors, while offering a temporary escape, ultimately create new problems that further complicate healing.

So, if you've experienced trauma, how do you find the support you need? The first step is acknowledging that you're not alone. There are countless resources available, from therapists specializing in trauma to support groups filled with understanding individuals who have walked a similar path.

Talking to a trusted friend or family member can also be a powerful first step. Sharing your experience, even in small pieces, can help break the isolation and begin the healing process. Remember, reaching out for help isn't a sign of weakness – it's a sign of strength.

Recovery from trauma is a journey, not a destination. There will be setbacks, but with the right support system in place, you can learn to heal and rebuild your life. You don't have to walk this path alone.

- Amanda Blackwood, human trafficking survivor.

Help Is Available

The weight of the world, it can feel like a ton,
Burdens we carry, 'til battles are won.

But sometimes, dear friend, the fight's best fought alone,
There's strength in seeking help, a path yet unknown.

A therapist's ear, a non-judgmental space,
To untangle the knots, with wisdom and grace.

To speak of the darkness, the fears and the shame,
And find in their presence, a comforting flame.

They hold up a mirror, reflecting us true,
The cracks and the scars, but the good shining through.

They teach us new tools, to navigate life's storm,
To weather the downpour, and weather the norm.

So don't be afraid, to take this brave leap,
For therapy's not weakness, it's secrets to keep.

It's learning to heal, and learning to grow,
A journey of self-love, where your spirit can flow.